T0068177

The Book of Proverbs

# Daily
# Affirmations
# and
# Prayers

Gale LeGrand Williams

WESTBOW
PRESS®
A DIVISION OF THOMAS NELSON
& ZONDERVAN

WestBow Press books may be ordered through booksellers or by contacting:

WestBow Press
A Division of Thomas Nelson & Zondervan
1663 Liberty Drive
Bloomington, IN 47403
www.westbowpress.com
844-714-3454

Scripture marked (NCV) taken from the New Century Version®. Copyright © 2005 by Thomas Nelson. Used by permission. All rights reserved.

Scripture marked (NKJV) taken from the New King James Version®. Copyright © 1982 by Thomas Nelson. Used by permission. All rights reserved.

ISBN: 978-1-6642-5227-1 (sc)
ISBN: 978-1-6642-5226-4 (e)

Library of Congress Control Number: 2021924871

Print information available on the last page.

WestBow Press rev. date: 2/7/2022

This book is dedicated to the "Women in New Direction" (WIND) dormitory at the Prince William County, Adult Detention Center.

"But if any of you needs wisdom, you should ask God for it. He is generous to everyone and will give you wisdom without criticizing you."

—James 1:5 (NCV)

*Bishop Gale LeGrand Williams*
*President and Founder*
*Entrusted Connections Ministry Inc.*

# CONTENTS

# INTRODUCTION

Reading a chapter from the book of Proverbs and speaking affirmations daily is a discipline I learned from women ex-offenders who were released from the "WIND" Dorm at the Adult Detention Center in Prince William County, Virginia, and who became residents of the Entrusted Connections Life House, a transitional home in Manassas, Virginia.

There is so much power that comes from reading one chapter from the book of Proverbs daily and the words of affirmations. The affirmations are verbal declarations of the Word of God, which provide comfort and confidence and bring about positive life changes.

I pray that as you read through this book of affirmations and prayers, you will experience the life-changing power of the Word of God over and into your life.

*"Wisdom is the principal thing; therefore, get wisdom. And in all your getting, get understanding." Proverbs 4:7 (NKJV)*

# CHAPTER 1

- I live by God's words of wisdom that empower me to reign in life. (v. 1)
- I am wise. I have self-control. I do what is honest, fair, and right. (v. 3)
- I have great skills to teach others to grow spiritually, and I share wisdom with them. (v. 4)
- I have wisdom that causes me to live with abundant blessings. (v. 5)
- I live in obedient devotion to God. (v. 7)
- I am attentive to the call of wise teaching. (v. 10)
- I walk in the way of goodness, and I stay on the path of righteousness. (v. 15)
- When wisdom calls, I will respond with obedience to her voice. (v. 20)
- Every decision that I make is to honor, respect, and worship God. (v. 29)
- The Spirit of God is upon me and causes me to know words of wisdom. (v. 23)
- Because I listen to the wisdom of God, I rest unafraid, and I am sheltered from the storms of life. (v. 33)

## NOTES

## CHAPTER 2

- Wisdom is a valuable treasure that I keep in my heart. (v. 1)
- I listen carefully to wisdom, and my mind is set to understand what I hear. (v. 2)
- I have full access to God's storehouse of wisdom, and I apply it to my life daily. (v. 7)
- As I follow God's plan, He guards my path and preserves my life. (v. 8)
- God protects me because I am loyal to Him. (v. 8)
- Discretion watches over me, and understanding keeps me safe. (v. 11)
- Wisdom keeps me in the company of good people who walk in the light of Christ. (vv. 12–13)
- I walk in the way of wisdom, and I stay on the paths of righteousness. (v. 20)
- Because I am a person of integrity, I enjoy life to the fullest. (v. 21)

### NOTES

## CHAPTER 3

- Because I have loyal love and faithfulness in my heart, I have favor and much success with God. (v. 3)
- I trust in the Lord completely, and He leads me in every decision that I make. (v. 5)
- Because I adore God with undivided devotion, my body is healthy, and my bones are strong. (vv. 7–8)
- I honor God with my financial increase, and every dimension of my life overflows with blessings. (vv. 9–10)
- I do not take the correction and discipline of the Lord lightly, because I know it comes from His passionate love for me. (vv. 11–12)
- Wisdom extends long life to me in one hand and wealth and promotion in the other. (v. 16)
- I will walk in wisdom, and I will discover my purpose so that I am strengthened and inspired to do what is right for my life. (vv. 21–22)
- God is my confidence in times of crisis, and He keeps my heart at rest in every situation. (v. 26)
- I will not avoid doing good to help someone when I am able to do so. (vv. 27–28)
- I have friendship with God, and I hear His intimate secrets. (v. 32)

### NOTES

# CHAPTER 4

- My heart retains God's Word, and I do not turn away from His instructions. (vv. 2, 4)
- I seek godly wisdom, and I do not forget or ignore the Word of God. (v. 5)
- I cling to wisdom for protection, and I love wisdom because it keeps me safe. (v. 6)
- The most important things I can do for my life are to seek spiritual discernment, mature comprehension, and godly interpretation of wisdom. (v. 7)
- I value the importance of wisdom for my life, and it makes me great. I embrace wisdom, and I receive a crown of honor. (vv. 8–9)
- Wisdom guides me and helps me to stay on the right path. My steps are not hindered, and I do not stumble. (vv. 11–12)
- I guard and protect wisdom, because the words of wisdom are my life. (v. 13)
- I do not follow the bad example of cruel and evil people. (v. 14)
- Wisdom guards me and keeps my heart and body protected. (vv. 22–23)
- I speak the truth, and I look straight ahead at wisdom. I do not turn aside to do evil. (vv. 24–25)

## NOTES

# CHAPTER 5

- I listen closely to wisdom; I have good judgment, and I always know the right things to say. (vv. 1–2)
- I use good judgment and godly wisdom. I am a morally credible person. (vv. 7–8)
- I will always live a life of honor and self-respect with a reputation for good deeds and discipline. (v. 9)
- My wealth will always remain in my house. My provisions will be used for my family. (v. 10)
- Not only do I give good advice, but I am also receptive to good advice. (v. 12)
- I will listen to the voices of my teachers and instructors of wisdom, and everything that I do brings glory to God. (vv. 13–14)
- I will be faithful and truthful in all my relationships. (v. 15)
- The Lord sees everything that I do. He is aware of every step that I take. (v. 21)
- Because I am righteous, I live a virtuous life. (v. 22)
- I will not stray from God's Word. I will receive godly instruction and live. (v. 23)

## NOTES

# CHAPTER 6

- I apply biblical principles to my finances. I avoid unnecessary debts. (vv. 1–2)
- I have learned wisdom from the ways of the ant. I am wise. I am resourceful. I have integrity. I work hard, and I have good judgment. (vv. 6–8)
- I am energetic. I have self-discipline. I prosper in all things. (vv. 9, 11)
- I am honest and truthful. I am a person of great value to my family and friends. (vv. 12–14)
- I have a heart for God and great hope for the future. I am righteous, and my soul is never shattered or damaged beyond repair. (v. 15)
- I do what God loves. I am humble and I am upright. I am charitable, and I am a peacemaker. (vv. 17–19)
- The wisdom of God leads, guides, and keeps me safe from harm throughout my day. (v. 22)
- The commandments of God are my lamp for my soul and a light for my path. Correction and self-control lead me to victory and a good life. (v. 23)
- I will preserve my life and my soul with righteous living and biblical standards. (vv. 32–33)

## NOTES

## CHAPTER 7

- I keep the commandments of God as a treasure that is always available to guide me. (v. 1)
- I guard the Word of God in my heart as a precious possession. I cannot live without it. (v. 2)
- I keep the words of God always before me as a constant reminder. They are written in my heart. (v. 3)
- I love wisdom like a sister, and I call understanding my close relative. (v. 4)
- Wisdom keeps me grounded; therefore, I am not swayed by flattery or sensual talk. (v. 5)
- I am not naive or foolish. I will not take the path that leads to seduction and lust. (vv. 7, 13–18)
- I will not allow the temptation to sin to have any success in my life. (v. 21)
- I will not only listen to the wisdom of God, I will obey. (v. 24)
- I will never leave the path of godly principles; I will not be misled or deceived by the enticement of sin. (v. 25)
- I will stand in awe of God and I will not sin against Him. (Chapter 7)

### NOTES

# CHAPTER 8

- I hear the call of wisdom and I listen to the voice of understanding. (v. 1)
- I understand wisdom and I have discipline that leads to godly living. (v. 5)
- My mouth speaks the truth. I refuse to speak otherwise. (v. 7)
- Every word that I speak is honest and full of goodness. (v. 8)
- The instructions that I receive from wisdom are more valuable to me than silver or gold. (v. 10)
- I respect and fear God, so I love what God loves. (v. 13)
- I love wisdom. I seek wisdom first before anything else and wisdom reveals herself to me. (v. 17)
- Because I love wisdom, I have wealth and great treasures. (v. 21)
- I am blessed and I have great joy because I follow the instructions of wisdom. (v. 32)
- What I learn from God's Word of wisdom is not in vain; what I know makes me wise. (v. 33)

## NOTES

# CHAPTER 9

- The home of wisdom is my dwelling place. (v. 1)
- I accept the rich provisions of understanding that I receive when I feast on the wisdom of God. (vv. 2–5)
- I will walk in the path of understanding and live a good life. (v. 6)
- As I receive wise instruction, I become wiser; and because I am righteous, when I acquire wisdom, I increase in knowledge. (v. 9)
- Because I want to become wise, I begin by respecting the Lord. As I come to know my Holy God, I will gain understanding. (v. 10)
- Because of the wisdom I receive from God, I will live a long time. Having wisdom adds years to my life. (v. 11)
- I will gain wisdom for my own good. I will seek knowledge for that which I do not understand. (v. 12)
- I am wise. I have great insight and keen understanding. (v. 13)
- I attract honesty. I welcome sincere people into my life. (v. 14)
- I find pleasure in my desire for holy, wholesome and healthy relationships. (v. 17)

## NOTES

# *Affirmations*

## CHAPTER 10

- My children are wise, and that makes me glad. (v. 1)
- Doing what is right saves my life and being honest brings me lasting happiness. (v. 2)
- Because I am righteous, the Lord nourishes my soul. (v. 3)
- Wealth comes to me because I work hard and I trust God. (v. 4)
- I am covered with the blessings of God. (v. 6)
- The memories that I leave will be a source of blessings. (v. 7)
- Because I am wise, I accept instructions easily. (v. 8)
- I am secure and confident because I walk in integrity and godly character. (v. 9)
- The blessings of the Lord bring true riches to my life and He adds no sorrow with it. (v. 22)
- The way of the Lord is a safe and strong resting place for me. (v. 29)

## NOTES

# *Affirmations*

## CHAPTER 11

- I have wisdom and soundness of mind because I have learned to walk humbly with God. (v. 2)
- Integrity guides my life and brings me success. I do what is right and I am honest in all that I do. (v. 3)
- Because I obey God, He saves my life. (v. 4)
- Because I am righteous, I live my life by being honest and having godly character. (v. 5)
- God delivers me from danger and trouble. (v. 8)
- I am trustworthy. I am a faithful confidante and friend. (v. 13)
- Because I have an abundance of wise and godly counsel, I am safe from harm. I have victory over the enemy. (v. 14)
- Because I am gracious and kind, I receive honor and I have a good reputation. (v. 16)
- I receive a lasting reward from God for the good that I do. (v. 18)
- Because I am righteous, my heart's desire is only for what is best, pleasing, and good. (v. 23)

## NOTES

# Affirmations

## CHAPTER 12

- I love the instruction that comes from my knowledge of wisdom. (v. 1)
- Because I am a good person, favor flows to me from the Lord. (v. 2)
- I am filled with good ideas that are righteous, noble, pure, and just. (v. 5)
- I am a person of wisdom and godly principles. (v. 8)
- I have what I need because I am a hard worker and I trust God. (v. 11)
- Because I love God, at the core of my heart, I am motivated by what is morally right (v. 12)
- I am teachable. I listen to wise counsel. (v. 15)
- I can be trusted, because I am a righteous person and I speak words of truth. (v. 17)
- I am filled with joy, because I always have a plan for peace. (v. 20)
- I choose my friends wisely! I have healthy relationships. (v. 26)

### NOTES

# *Affirmations*

## CHAPTER 13

- I love God, I love truth and honesty. (v. 5)
- I am a person of integrity. Righteousness is my shield of protection. (v. 6)
- Because I love God, my inner light grows brighter in dark places and brings me joy. (v. 9)
- My wealth increases because I gather it by my labor and not dishonestly. (v. 11)
- God rewards me because I honor and respect His Holy Word. (v. 13)
- I am a trustworthy and wise messenger of God. I bring health and healing wherever I go. (v. 17)
- I accept correction. I walk in the path of honor. (v. 18)
- I will spend time with people who are wise so that I can grow in wisdom. (v. 20)
- I will leave an inheritance to my children's children. As a righteous person I will receive the stored-up wealth of sinners. (v. 22)
- God satisfies my soul with more than enough. (v. 25)

### NOTES

# *Affirmations*

## CHAPTER 14

- I am wise. I encourage and build up my family. (v. 1)
- I love and fear the Lord. I follow His path of integrity for my life. (v.2)
- I am a faithful person and a truthful witness. (v. 5)
- Because I need wise counsel, I keep company with people who are knowledgeable. (v. 7)
- I am a person of wisdom. I invite good into my life. My confidence remains in God. (v. 16)
- I am prosperous. I am blessed. I am kind to the poor. (v. 21)
- Because I make plans for good things in my life, mercy and truth are my trusted companions. (v. 22)
- Because I am wise, God rewards me with more wisdom. (v. 24)
- I am patient and slow to anger. My heart is full of great understanding for others. (v. 29)
- My body is full of life and health, because my heart and mind are full of peace. (v. 30)

## NOTES

# *Affirmations*

## CHAPTER 15

- My gentle response turns away anger and rage. (v. 1)
- I will use my words to foster healing to fix the problem and not add blame. (v. 4)
- I am teachable. I receive correction with a humble heart. (v. 5)
- I choose to be happy every day. (v. 15)
- I am calm and patient. I am a peace-maker and I live in peace. (v. 18)
- I have given myself to understand wisdom. I make good choices for my life. (v. 21)
- I get good advice and wise counsel, and I watch my plans succeed. (v. 22)
- I give appropriate answers with joy. I speak good words at the right time. (v. 23)
- God stirs my heart before I speak. He fills my mouth with right answers. (v. 28)
- I surrender myself to instructions of wisdom. I humble myself as I receive honor from the Lord. (v. 33)

## NOTES

*Affirmations*

# CHAPTER 16

- I await answers from the Lord to confirm the preparations of my heart (v. 1)
- I trust God to test and reveal the motives of my heart so that His purposes will be established in my life. (vv. 23)
- God forgives my sins and I follow His righteous paths for my life. (v. 6)
- Because I live to please God, He gives me favor and I live in peace with all people. (v. 7)
- All my steps are directed by the Lord. (v. 9)
- God sets my standards for righteousness to be fair and honest in all that I do. (v. 11)
- I will preserve my soul with holy and righteous living. (v. 17)
- Because I am humble, I walk uprightly before God. (v. 18)
- Because I trust God, I am blessed. (v. 20)
- I speak life giving words that bring health and healing to the bones of others. (v. 24)

## NOTES

# CHAPTER 17

- I live a humble life. My home is full of peace and quiet (v. 1)
- The Lord uses tests and trials to purify my heart while He removes impurities. It is the same way that fire refines silver and gold. (v. 3)
- My ears are open to words that encourage and uplift my spirit. (v. 4)
- The love of God in my heart makes me quick to forgive offenses directed at me by others. (v. 9)
- I return good for evil; therefore, good will never depart from my home. (v. 13)
- I am blessed that I can depend on the love of my friends at all times. (v. 17)
- I am grateful to God to have a family that sticks with me no matter what storms come into my life. (v. 17)
- I love peace and I live humbly with my God. (v. 19)
- My happy heart is the medicine that brings health and healing to my body and soul. (v. 22)
- My knowledge of godly wisdom provides me the understanding I need to be cool, calm, and collected no matter what I am facing. (v. 27)

## NOTES

# *Affirmations*

## CHAPTER 18

- I am friendly. I make myself available to attend to the needs of others. (v. 1)
- I listen to learn wisdom. I give my attention to hear the voice of others. (v. 2)
- I am fair and just to all people. (v. 5)
- The name of the Lord is my go-to place for safety and protection. He keeps me secure. (v. 10)
- I humble myself before the Lord and receive honor from His hands. (v. 12)
- My heart acquires knowledge. My ears are always open to learn more. (v. 15)
- My gifts make room for me and bring me before great people. (v. 16)
- The wisdom that comes from my mouth empowers the lives of others. (v. 20)
- The fruit of my lips speak life and not death. (v. 21)
- Because I am friendly, I am surrounded by friends. My loyal friends are like family to me. (v. 24)

## NOTES

# *Affirmations*

## CHAPTER 19

- I walk in integrity because I obtain Divine wisdom, knowledge, and instruction from God. (vv.1–2)
- I love godly wisdom. I learn all that I can, and as a result I am prosperous. I experience good success. (v. 8)
- I am patient and not easily angered. I am quick to forgive offenses and insults. (v. 11)
- I keep God's commandments and I honor His instructions. (v. 16)
- I give freely to the poor. My reward comes from God. (v. 17)
- I listen to wise advice, which causes me to live wisely and well. (v. 20)
- I make plans for my life, but I know God's purposes for me will succeed in the end. (v. 21)
- My heart desires to be kind to all people. (v. 22)
- Because I fear God, I live in peace and I can rest. He keeps me safe from harm. (v. 23)
- I honor and cherish my parents, and I make them proud that I am their child. (v. 26)

## NOTES

# *Affirmations*

## CHAPTER 20

- I walk in wisdom. I am disciplined. I have self-control. (v. 1)
- I am a person of honor and peace. (v. 3)
- I have a deep well of wisdom in my heart and it is drawn out like water to provide counsel to those who need good advice. (v. 5)
- Because I am righteous and walk in integrity, I am a blessing to my children. (v. 7)
- God has formed my eyes to see His beauty and made my ears to hear His voice. (v. 12)
- My friends and associates are people of integrity. (v. 19)
- I wait on God. The good He has for my life always prevails. (v. 22)
- I keep my vows that I make to God. (v. 25)
- My spirit is the lamp of the Lord inside of me. God searches the intents of my heart. (v. 27)

## NOTES

*Affirmations*

# CHAPTER 21

- The Lord knows my heart and confirms the way that I take. (v. 2)
- I do what is right, and I am fair and just with others, which pleases God more than any sacrifices to Him. (v. 3)
- I take time to think things through. I am diligent and work hard, which leads me to prosperity and plenty. (v. 5)
- I am wise and teachable, and I receive knowledge from wise instruction. (v. 11)
- I keep my ears open to hear the needs of the poor. (v.13)
- Because I am wise, my home is blessed by God. (v. 20)
- I follow after righteousness and mercy; therefore, in God's grace, I find life, righteousness, and honor. (v. 21)
- I guard my mouth and I am careful with what I say; that way, I stay out of trouble. (v. 23)
- I give generously to those in need (vv. 25–26)
- In every battle that I face, I know my deliverance and victory comes from the Lord (v. 31)

## NOTES

*Affirmations*

# CHAPTER 22

- Having a good name with loving favor is more important to me than having riches. (v. 1)
- I have riches and honor because I fear and reverence God. (v. 4)
- I value my soul and I know what is good for me. (v. 5)
- Because I am generous to the poor, I am blessed in return. (v. 9)
- I live in peace, and love fills my home with kindness and gentleness (v. 10)
- I pay attention to what I am taught. I hold onto wisdom and I speak wisdom appropriately. (vv. 17-18)
- Because I have received instruction in wisdom, I trust in God. (v. 19)
- My friends are loving and kind. They lead me by their examples. (vv. 24–25)
- I live by Biblical principles of finances. I stay out of debt. (vv. 26–27)
- I am excellent and gifted in my work. I will be promoted. I will stand in the presence of great leaders. (v. 29)

## NOTES

# CHAPTER 23

- I control my appetite. I consider my manners when I receive an invitation to share a meal with others. (vv. 1, 6–7)
- I accept God's wisdom for my life. He gives me the wisdom and power to obtain wealth. (v. 4)
- I spend my time with people who love the wisdom of God. (v. 9)
- I will pay close attention to words of instruction and correction for my life. I will open my ears to words of knowledge. (v. 12)
- My heart is full of wisdom and I speak words that are right and good. (vv. 15–16)
- My true passion is the fear and respect I have for the Lord. My hope and my future rest in God. (vv. 17–18)
- I make right decisions because I listen to words of wisdom and they guide my life. (v. 19)
- I treasure the word of God, and I embrace and hold close to my heart wisdom, instruction, and understanding (v. 23)
- I respect my parents. I am attentive to their needs. I make them proud of me because I have chosen to live a godly and righteous life. (vv. 22, 24–25)
- I enjoy the company of those who love God and have an appreciation for the things of God. (vv. 30–31)

## NOTES

# *Affirmations*

## CHAPTER 24

- I admire people with a good heart. I enjoy spending time with them. (v. 1)
- My home is built through wisdom. I have understanding as my foundation. My rooms are filled with knowledge and spiritual riches of God's grace. (vv. 3-4)
- Because I am wise, I have great power. Because I know the Word of God, I have increased stability. (v. 5)
- I have great strength and courage to overcome adversity. (v. 10)
- Wisdom is sweet like honey to me. I have found it. Now I have a hope and a future that will not be cut off. (vv. 13–14)
- Because I love God, I will continue to rise again and again. (v. 16)
- I will humble my heart and pray for God's goodness when my enemy falls or stumbles. (vv. 17–18)
- I walk in power, love and a sound mind. I appreciate the kindness of good people. (v. 19)
- I am fair and righteous in my thoughts of others. (v. 23)
- I speak honestly so that I can win the hearts of people. (v. 26)

## NOTES

*Affirmations*

# CHAPTER 25

- I humble myself at all times. I allow the favor of God to put me in places of honor. (vv. 6–7)
- I have a reputation for being a friend who can be trusted with secrets. (vv. 9–10)
- The words that I speak are as valuable as apples of gold in settings of silver. (v. 11)
- I humbly receive wise correction and it gives beauty to my life. It makes me a better person. (v. 12)
- I am faithful and dependable. I am a breath of fresh air to those who trust me. (v. 13)
- I am patient and speak with gentle words. The hearts of those in authority are persuaded to change. (v. 15)
- I respect the privacy of my friends and neighbors, and they enjoy my visits. (v. 17)
- I feed my enemy when he is hungry. I give him drink for his thirst. God rewards me for my kindness. (vv. 21–22)
- I am humbled when I receive praises from others. (v. 27)
- I am a person of self-control and structure. I rule my life with obedience to God. (v. 28)

## NOTES

# *Affirmations*

## CHAPTER 26

- I am a person of wisdom and I speak words of wisdom. (vv. 4–5)
- I am humble and I accept God's will for my life. (v. 12)
- I seek wise counsel for sensible answers. (v. 16)
- I am a keeper of peace. I speak words of peace. (v. 17)
- I am an honest and trustworthy friend. (v. 19)
- I am a great companion and confidante to my friends. I am a peacemaker. (vv. 20–21)
- I am a lover of truth. I use words of praise to encourage others. (vv. 24–25)
- I always look for ways to be a blessing. (v. 27)

## NOTES

*Affirmations*

# CHAPTER 27

- I will humble myself and keep my heart from pride. (v. 2)
- I trust the correction of a wise and faithful loved one. (v. 6)
- My heart receives joy from the good advice of my friends; it's like the sweet fragrance of choice perfumes in my nostrils. (v. 9)
- The friends who are close to me are more available to me in my time of need than relatives who are far away. (v. 10)
- I am wise. I remove myself from dangerous and troublesome situations. (v. 12)
- My friends and I encourage each other to love and to do good works, making us the iron that sharpens iron. (v. 17)
- The words, actions, and intentions of my heart are true reflections of who I am. (v. 19)
- I am content with what I have. (v. 20)
- The purity of my heart reveals my thankfulness to God. (v. 21)
- I work hard. I am careful with what God provides for me. I will always have plenty for my future. (vv. 23–27)

## NOTES

# *Affirmations*

## CHAPTER 28

- Since I am in right standing with God, I trust Him at all times. I am confident, relaxed, and bold as a lion. (v.1)
- I am obedient to the laws of God. My associations are with like-minded people. (v. 4)
- I am fully devoted to God. I completely understand the importance of justice. (v. 5)
- I am wise. I obey God's law. I do not make friends with troublemakers or disgrace my family. (v. 7)
- I hear and obey God's instructions. His ears are open to my prayers. (v. 9)
- I confess and turn from my sins and I receive mercy from God. (v. 13)
- My life is blessed because I respect and I obey God. (v. 14)
- I walk in integrity and uprightly with God. He keeps me safe and He delivers me from harm. (v. 18)
- I work hard and I am intentional in planning my future. I have plenty. (v. 19)
- Because I give to the poor, God supplies my needs and I lack nothing. (v. 27)

## NOTES

# *Affirmations*

## CHAPTER 29

- I humble myself and accept God's correction in my life. (v. 1)
- I love wisdom. I am prudent with my wealth. I bring great pleasure to my family and friends. (v. 3)
- I align myself with those whose interest is doing what is right and fair for the poor. (v. 7)
- I walk in the wisdom of God. I am a peacemaker and l restore order. (v. 8)
- I am patient and I control my emotions because I walk in the wisdom of God. (v. 11)
- I am slow to speak. I choose my words carefully. (v. 20)
- I obtain honor from God with a meek and humble spirit. (v. 23)
- I trust God. I am safe. I walk in the freedom of having the perfect love of God in my life. (v. 25)
- The justice that I need for my life comes from God. (v. 26)
- My honest and upright way of life is an encouragement to righteous people. (v. 27)

## NOTES

# *Affirmations*

## CHAPTER 30

- I am made in the image of God. I comprehend great things. (v. 2)
- I have received the revelation of truth and wisdom. God has made His Holiness known to me. (v. 3)
- All of God's words are true and pure. He guards me. He keeps me safe. (v. 5)
- I love the Word of God. I am not wise above what is written. (v. 6)
- I am not ashamed of God. I honor the power of His name. (v. 9)
- I am humble. I am meek. I do not think more highly of myself than I think of others. (v. 13)
- I am exceedingly wise. I have plenty and I know no want; I go to "The Rock" for my shelter and support. I have good order in my life. I combine excellence and faithfulness into my life regardless of difficulties that I face. (vv. 24–28)
- Like a lion is without fear, I am bold and courageous in my service for Christ. (v. 30)
- I release peace and bring a calm spirit with me everywhere I go. (v. 33)

## NOTES

## CHAPTER 31

- I will speak up for those who cannot speak for themselves. I will defend the rights of those who are defenseless. (v. 7)
- I am a person of excellence. My worth exceeds the value of fine jewels. (v. 10)
- I do good and I am kind every day of my life. (v. 12)
- I am a wise and prudent business person. I use my profits to benefit my household. (v. 16)
- I reach out to the needy. I give generously to the poor. (v. 20)
- I am a person of strength and honor. I am joyful for the future. (v. 25)
- When I speak my words are wise and kindness covers everything that I say. (v. 26)
- I take good care of my household. I watch over everything that happens there. I enjoy the fruit of my labor. (v. 27)
- Because I love and honor God, I receive approval and admiration from others. (v. 30)
- I will be rewarded for the work I have done. My good works will bring me honor and recognition from all people. (v. 31)

### NOTES

# Prayers

# PRAYER OF PROTECTION

*Most Holy Father, bless this day, be with me, and let Your angels protect me from dangers seen and unseen. I thank You that because of my faith in You, You continue to allow me to see the power of the cross in my life: healing, deliverance, and abundant life. Grant me Your favor today—favor with You and favor with all those with whom I interact. Grant me Your peace today, and give me comfort when I find myself in places of confusion and stress. Help me to forgive others as You have forgiven me. Let me be quick to be generous with my resources, and at the end of today, let me remember that because of Your grace, because of Your mercy, and because of Your love, You gave me victory over every plot, plan, and scheme of the enemy. I am grateful for all Your many blessings, and I thank You for calling me Your own. In the powerful name of Jesus Christ, I pray. Amen.*

# PRAYER FOR WISDOM

*Father, I thank You for the wisdom You give me on a daily basis—the wisdom to be righteous, the wisdom to know when to speak and when to remain silent, and the wisdom to know when to pray and when to move by Your grace. I thank You for Your liberal and generous wisdom that is sufficient for every situation that I face, that guides me in victory over the enemy of my soul; Your wisdom that allows me to have inner peace that keeps me in a place of rest. Thank you for the peace with others that allows me to live in unity with family, friends, and those I come in contact with.*

*I thank You, Father, for Your protection and for Your angels who surround me every day to keep me safe from hurt, harm, and danger. I thank You, Father, for working all things together for my good.*

*I thank You, Father, for continuing to grant me the blessings of Psalm 91 and Deuteronomy 28, today and forever. In Jesus's name, I pray. Amen.*

# PRAYER OF VICTORY

*Most Holy Father, I thank You that on this day I will walk in victory. I know that any battle that I face does not belong to me; every battle is Yours. Help me to be still so that I can see and experience You rescue me from my enemies. I will not fear, because I know that You are with me. I will not fear, because I have Your perfect love within me that casts out all fear. Your Word says You give me victory through Jesus Christ, and as Your child my faith is what gives me this victory. So, on today I walk in faith for every victory. On today I walk as an overcomer. On today I have faith in You, Father, and no fear. On today I will walk in Your perfect love. I decree and declare that no weapon formed against me shall prosper, and I will see Your glory upon my life. I will speak Your Word to every mountain and obstacle, and by my faith in You I know You are going to make a way for me to overcome. I decree and declare victory on this day.*

*In the precious name of Jesus Christ, I pray. Amen.*

# PRAYER FOR HEALING

*Father I thank You for the finished work of Jesus Christ on the cross. I thank you that You are with me, that You love me, and that You are my very present help. Father I thank You that my body is healed and restored; I am being transformed every day that I come into Your presence. I speak healing and restoration in my body according to Your Word.*

*Lord, look upon me with Your eyes of mercy. May Your healing virtue rest upon me, may Your healing powers flow into every cell of my body, into my immune system, and into the depths of my soul; bring health to my flesh, cleansing and restoring me to wholeness and strength for service in Your Kingdom by the blood that You shed on the cross. I decree and declare there is no one like You, no one can compare to You. I trust you, Father, for the healing that I need and for the healing that I pray for others. I trust You, Father, and I thank You for Your daily blessings in my life. In Jesus's name, I pray. Amen.*

# PRAYER FOR RIGHT THINKING

*Father, you said in your Word that I should think on what is true and good and right. You said I should think about things that are pure and lovely, and dwell on good things in others; and when I do that, Your peace will be with me. Father, help me to know that I can choose my thoughts, help me to fix my mind on those things that will keep me from stress and confusion. Father, help me to remember that as I think on what is true, good, and right, and when I think good things about others You are transforming my life to become a person of integrity and honor, helping me to forget the old negative things in my past and reach for the good that You have for my future. Father, help me to not be so familiar with my salvation and Your grace that I take you for granted. Restore the joy of my salvation, the excitement I once had for You and about You. Give me a renewed joy in knowing You. Help me to get excited again. In Jesus's name, I pray. Amen.*

# PRAYER OF TRUSTING GOD

*Father, on this day I decree and declare that my trust is in You, and I will trust You. You said in Your Word that if I trust You, You will be my shield and my protector. Your Word says You will save me from violence, Your Word says You will give me victory in my battles. Your Word says I am to pour out my heart before You because You are a place of safety for me. When the doctor says disease and infirmities, I trust You for healing; when the bank says no to the loan, I trust You for provision. So, Father, I trust You for guidance and deliverance. I will trust You with all of my heart, and I will not lean on my own understanding. I will acknowledge You in everything that I do so that You will direct my path—paths that are righteous, so that Your name will be glorified in my life. Father, let Your angels surround me, and may the peace of the Holy Spirit give me an assurance that all is well and good things shall be my portion! In Jesus's name. Amen.*

# PRAYER OF THANKSGIVING

*Most Holy and Righteous Father, I come before You on today with a heart full of thanksgiving. I thank You for life, health, and strength. I thank You for Your faithfulness and Your love. Father, I thank You that You hear me and You answer my prayers. I thank You, Father, that the legacy of peace that Jesus left for us will continue to manifest in this nation. Let us all live in peace. Father, keep me safe today. Thank You for Your favor that rests upon my life, remember those I love and allow them to experience the same grace that You give to me in their lives today. Father, I know that You love me; help me to love others as You love me. I thank You, Father, for defeating the enemy in my life on today at every turn. Let the enemy withdraw from me each day as he did with Jesus in the wilderness. Lord Jesus, thank You for healing me. I decree and declare that today I will walk in victory, I will walk in Divine healing, I will walk in favor, and I will walk in love. I pray this Prayer of Thanksgiving in Jesus's name. Amen.*

# PRAYER TO BE TRUSTWORTHY

*Most Holy Father, on today I come before You asking that You help me to be trustworthy today—worthy of Your trust for the things that You have entrusted to my care and worthy of the trust of others. Help me not to be careless when I speak Your Word, help me to be faithful to what You have assigned to my hands, help me to be kind and love as You have loved me, help me be quick to forgive, help me to share the burdens of my friends and loved ones, and help me to be true to who I am in You. Father, help me to be a person of integrity and honesty. Help me to be quick to encourage and slow to criticize. Have compassion on me, Father, and help me as I go throughout this day. Father, let my heart be full of Your joy, and let the words of my mouth and the thoughts that I think be acceptable to You. Help me to be a worthy representative of You on this day, and make me a vessel fit for Your use. Thank You Father for loving me. In Jesus's name, I pray. Amen.*

# PRAYER FOR GOD'S GUIDANCE

*Father, I lift my eyes to the hills from where I receive help when my heart is overwhelmed by the pressures of life. I am grateful that You call me Your own. Father, on this day I pray that You will lead me and guide me; that Your hand of protection will be with me. Father, Your Word says, "You will instruct me and teach me in the way I should go; You said You will guide me with Your eye." Father, I know that You have a plan for me, so as I walk through this day with You, let me hear Your word saying to me, "This is the way, walk in it." Father, keep me from the desire to control my own destiny or walk in the desire of my own heart. Help me to be Your faithful follower, one of Your humble sheep, so that at the end of this day I will not be regretful of my disobedience to You, but I will say in my heart, all has been well with me, and God has guided me and provided me with His goodness and His truth. Lead me to good works and faithful service to You. In Jesus's name, I pray. Amen.*

# PRAYER OF COMFORT

*God of Comfort, my heart is sorrowful on today. I need to feel Your presence in my life; draw me close to You. I need You to heal my broken heart. Father, You said You are a very present help in the time of trouble. You are the God of all power, and no one and nothing can stand in defiance in Your presence. I surrender my anxieties to You, and I will be still and realize that You are God and God alone and You will comfort me. You will heal my pain. You will restore my joy, and You will give me that peace that is difficult for me to understand but easy for me to accept. I know You are near to the brokenhearted and You save those who are crushed in spirit. I thank You Father, that You will deliver me from every affliction in my mind, soul, body, and spirit. I will not be defeated by the spirit of fear of loss and loneliness, but I will walk in Your perfect love. Thank You, Father, for Your comfort on today. In the name of Jesus, I will rejoice and be glad. Amen.*

For more information on Entrusted Connections Ministry or Bishop Gale LeGrand Williams go to www.ec-ministry.com.

Also by Gale LeGrand Williams:
Lovingkindness in the Morning
(A 366 Day Devotional)

Printed in the United States
by Baker & Taylor Publisher Services